you are a

WORLD CHANGER

21-Day Kids' Devotional

Written By: Kimberly & Caleb Rankin
Illustrated By: Caleb Rankin

World Changer: 21-Day Kids' Devotional
Written by Kimberly & Caleb Rankin
Illustrated by Caleb Rankin
Special Thanks to Sarah Logan

CAMP TOWN

CAMPTOWNMEDIA.COM

Get Ready to
CHANGE YOUR WORLD!

HOW TO USE THIS DEVOTIONAL

Welcome to **YOUR** devotional! That's right! It's completely yours. You are encouraged to read it, write in it and spend time with it each day.

This is a **FIELD GUIDE** to learn how to change your world, so keep it close-by! You never know when it'll come in handy.

The key to getting the most out of this devotional is to use it **EVERY DAY.** If you are a "get-up early" kid, that's awesome! Read it when you first get up to start off your day. If you are a "stay-up late" kid, that's super cool, too. Read it right before you go to bed at night. Whatever time you choose is perfect for you.

Be sure to have a pencil, a pen, or lots of pencils and pens with you to write on the pages. Also make sure to keep your **BIBLE** or a Bible App handy. Some of the verses are printed in this devotional, but you will need to look others up.

Each day you will focus on one idea to help you be a 100% awesome World Changer. The devotion will have thoughts and verses to read, things for you to write or do, plus a daily **WORLD CHANGER CHALLENGE**.

Some challenges are easy and can be done quickly. Some require more thinking and creativity, and may take a more time. But you're up for the challenge, right?

Though this is a daily devotional, it's also divided into three weeks, or three stages for becoming the World Changer God has called you to be. Let's take a look at those weeks.

The **FIRST WEEK** is all about **YOU!** Yes, you! Your heart, the way you think, attitudes, and more. Being an effective World Changer starts with you.

The **SECOND WEEK** is all about **YOUR ATMOSPHERE**; areas closest to you. Your parents, siblings, friends, and places you go the most. This will help you start changing the world you most live in and relationships that are important to you.

In the **THIRD WEEK** you will focus on the bigger world around you, your city, state, country and, of course, **THE WORLD!** We weren't kidding when we said **YOU ARE A WORLD CHANGER!**

IMPORTANT THINGS TO REMEMBER...

Some devotions might come easy to you and you will master the concept right away. Others may take more work. This is your devotional. You can read and read and read pages again and again if you like.

You also need to know that changing the world takes time. You can't just do a challenge and say "All done!" Repeating the lessons and the things you've learned until they become a habit will help you become an effective World Changer.

YOU CAN DO IT!

YOU CAN MAKE THE WORLD A BETTER PLACE.

YOU ARE A WORLD CHANGER!!

> We are God's masterpiece. He has created us anew in Christ Jesus, so we can do the good things he planned for us long ago.
> Ephesians 2:10

You are a **WORLD CHANGER** for sure and God has **BIG PLANS** just for you . How cool is that?

You were made on purpose and with a purpose, but you don't have to do it alone.

God wants you to talk to him about areas that are challenging to you. He wants to help you become the best World Changer you can be. It is so important to **TALK TO GOD** at the end of each devotion and ask Him for his help.

You might have to talk to God over and over again about the same topic. That's alright! God is so excited to help you **CHANGE THE WORLD!!**

Before you start, take a moment and ask God to open up your heart and to get you ready for the things you will learn and the challenges you will take.

Excited for this adventure? You should be...you are 21 days away from being a **KID WHO CHANGES THE WORLD!!**

OK, TURN THE PAGE & LET'S GET STARTED!

HELLO WORLD CHANGER! Yep, that's you. You, right now, are chosen to be a World Changer! Isn't that exciting? You will spend the next 21 days actively making the world more awesome! Ready to get started? Let's do it!

First, let's look at *your* world, starting with...

YOU

My name is _____.

I am _____ years old and I am already a **WORLD CHANGER!!**

I want to be a _____ when I grow up.

My favorite thing right now is _____.

Great start! Now let's go to **YOUR FAMILY!**

My family has _____ people and _____ pets.

My family is awesome because _____

_____.

IN THE SPACE BELOW DRAW A PICTURE OF YOUR FAMILY & INCLUDE YOUR PETS!

MY FAMILY

You are doing great! Now let's expand your world a little further and talk about **YOUR SCHOOL!**

I am in _____ grade at_____.

I have _____ kids in my class.

My teacher's name is _____.

Use the box below to write what you love about your school.

AMAZING JOB! Almost done! Now let's think about all the other places you spend time. Do you play a sport or are you on a team? What about an after school club or group? Use the space below to make a list of all the other places you spend time. Those places are part of your world too!

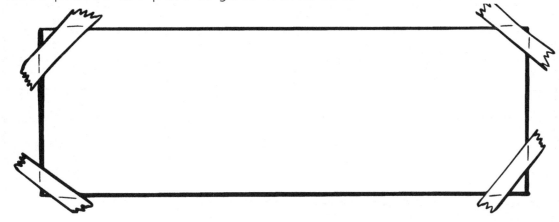

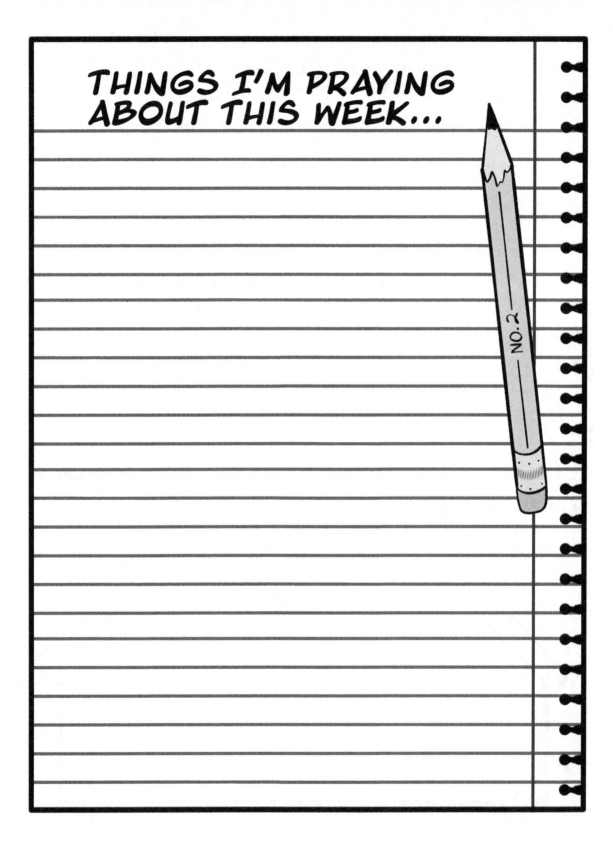

WEEK 1
CHANGE YOUR HEART

This week you will start changing the world by...

- [ ] Changing your **HEART**
- [ ] Changing your **PRIORITIES**
- [ ] Changing your **ATTITUDE**
- [ ] Changing your **MIND**
- [ ] Changing your **WORDS**
- [ ] Changing your **ACTIONS**
- [ ] Putting on your **ARMOR**

WELCOME TO DAY #1!

Today is a great day! Did you know that God created you on purpose, and with a purpose? Yep, right now, at the age you are God has a plan just for **YOU!** You are a World Changer!

But how can you change the world? First we must look inside ourselves. ***TODAY'S FOCUS IS ABOUT YOU AND YOUR HEART.*** Here are some places to start.

DO YOU BELIEVE...

...ALL THE BIBLE IS TRUE?

It is! It is God's Word for us. It's like God wrote a big letter to you about how much He loves you and cares for you. Check out 2 Timothy 3:16; *"All Scripture is inspired by God and is useful to teach us what is true and to make us realize what is wrong in our lives."*

...JESUS IS GOD'S SON?

God loves us so much that He sent his son, Jesus to bring us a very special gift; Eternal Life. In fact, John 3:16 says exactly that; *"For God loved the world so much that he gave his one and only Son, so that everyone who believes in him will not perish but have eternal life."*

...THAT YOU HAVE SINNED?

Sin is anything we do, say, or even think that disobeys God's Word. And the Bible says that everyone sins. We all miss the mark. Sadly, our sin separates us from being God's friend. Look at Romans 3:23, *"Everyone has sinned; we all fall short of God's glorious standard."* But that's why Jesus came to earth; to die on the Cross for our sins.

...THAT JESUS DIED FOR YOUR SINS?

Have you ever traded with someone? When Jesus died on the Cross he made a way for us to make the best trade ever! He got the punishment for our sins and we get forgiveness and a friendship with God. How cool is that! Read what Romans 5:8. *"But God showed his great love for us by sending Christ to die for us while we were still sinners."*

...THAT YOUR SINS CAN BE FORGIVEN?

They CAN! The Bible tells us in Romans 10:9 exactly how, *"If you confess with your mouth that Jesus is Lord and believe in your heart that God raised him from the dead, you will be saved."*

If you've already asked Jesus to forgive you of your sins and come into your heart, **THAT'S AWESOME!** You are already on your way to becoming a World Changer!

But if you haven't, **TODAY** can be that day! Before you can change the world you must first change your heart. Sin hardens your heart like a stone, but asking Jesus to forgive your sins makes your heart brand new and clean. Listen to this. *"Anyone who belongs to Christ has become a new person. The old life is gone; a new life has begun!"* -2 Corinthians 5:17

WORLD CHANGER CHALLENGE: Is today the day you want to become a brand new person? If so, let's follow the ABC's!
- **A**=Admit you have sinned.
- **B**=Believe Jesus is the son of God and he died on the Cross for your sins, and rose from the dead.
- **C**=Confess with your mouth. This is just talking to God, which is called prayer. You can use the prayer on the next page as an example.

PRAY THIS PRAYER OUT LOUD!

Dear God,

I know I have sinned and that sin separates me from you. You loved me so much that you sent your Son, Jesus to die on the Cross and take the punishment that my sins deserved. I believe that Jesus died on the Cross for my sins, and that he rose from the dead. Please forgive me for all my sins and make my heart brand new. Help me to love you and follow you every day of my life. Thank you for your love and for your kindness to me.

Amen!

Guess what?
Now you are a **CHRISTIAN!!**
That is so awesome!
You are now best friends with God!

TODAY your heart is brand new so it is like a birthday for your heart! Write down today's date in the space below so you can always remember this day. And be sure to tell your family so they can celebrate with you too! If you've already asked Jesus into your heart, write the date or your age when you did.

I ASKED JESUS INTO MY HEART...

_____

SING A CHORUS OF HAPPY BIRTHDAY AND CELEBRATE THIS AMAZING DECISION.

Use the space below to write a thank you letter to Jesus or draw how you feel knowing your sins are forgiven.

HELLO WORLD CHANGER!
IT'S DAY #2

Today is a wonderful day and you will do awesome things! You are a World Changer!

As we continue learning how we can change the world by letting God change us, we are going to learn about our **PRIORITIES.** Priorities is a fancy word for things that are important to us. Make a list in the space below of some things in your life that are **SUPER IMPORTANT** to you.

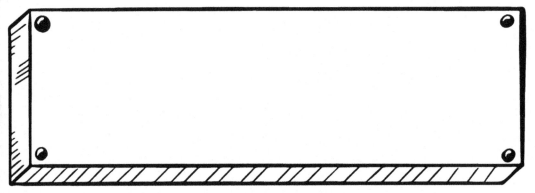

When we commit to love Jesus with all of our heart, we make Jesus the Lord of our lives, which means we put him in charge of us! We listen to him and follow what He says, and he takes care of us! Write down three people who also take care of you.

1.

2.

3.

WHEN WE MAKE JESUS OUR LORD WE ARE SAYING THAT WHAT IS IMPORTANT TO JESUS IS ALSO NOW IMPORTANT TO US.

WHAT ARE SOME THINGS YOU THINK ARE IMPORTANT TO JESUS?

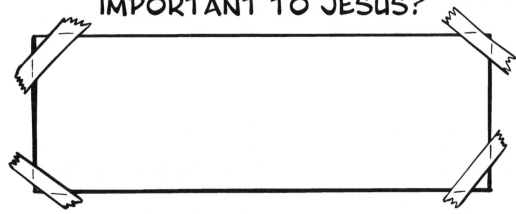

Matthew 22:37-39 tells us the most important thing to Jesus. **"Jesus replied, 'You must love the Lord your God with all your heart, all your mind, and all your soul.' This is the first and greatest commandment. A second is equally important: 'Love your neighbor as yourself.'"**

That verse is actually the key to becoming a World Changer. Loving God and loving others sets our priorities right and empowers us to change the world!

WORLD CHANGER CHALLENGE: Think about your family. Write an idea in the space below of something you can do to show love to someone in your family.

IT'S DAY #3 OF BEING A WORLD CHANGER!

Today is the **BEST!** You are changing the world!! And God is helping change your heart. God has big plans for you to change your world, and a big part of that is allowing God to change us from the inside, out.

Ready to start? Today we are looking at **OUR ATTITUDES!**

Use the space below to write about times you have had a **GOOD ATTITUDE** towards someone or something.

Now write about some times you have had a **BAD ATTITUDE** towards someone or something.

WHY DOES OUR ATTITUDE MATTER SO MUCH?

Because we want to be followers of Jesus and Jesus sets the best example for us to follow. Can you guess what kind of attitude Jesus had? Check out the verse on the next page!

"Imitate God, therefore, in everything you do, because you are his dear children. Live a life filled with love, following the example of Christ."
Ephesians 5:1-2a

Grab your Bible and read this story in **JOHN 13:1-17** to see Jesus' example in action.

Jesus served his disciples. He saw something that needed to be done and he did it. All with a **GREAT ATTITUDE.**

WORLD CHANGER CHALLENGE: Think about the people in your world. How can you follow Jesus' example and serve them? Use the chart below to help you think of ideas.

Who can I serve?	What I can do to serve them?

HEY THERE, WORLD CHANGER!
IT'S DAY #4

It is an amazing day! Right now, where you are, say this out loud..."*I AM A WORLD CHANGER!*" You are created by God to do amazing things, right now! You don't have to wait until you grow up to change your world! Isn't that amazing?

Today the focus is on **OUR MINDS.** Our minds are like super-computers that can store lots of stuff, like what we had for breakfast, what our favorite color is and how we feel about broccoli! But how does that information get into our minds?

With a **CRAYON** color in the box that says **COLOR HERE**. Fill it completely solid. Press **HARD** with the crayon. Then carefully fold this page over and rub the colored-in box with the blank box.

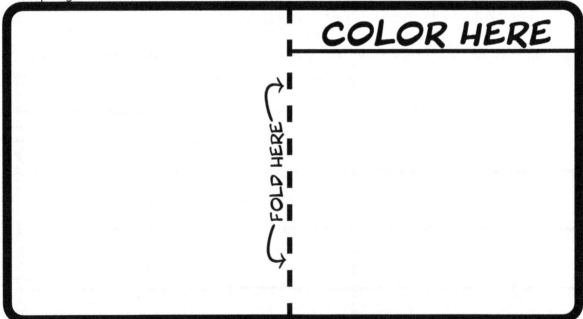

COLOR HERE

FOLD HERE

DID THE COLOR RUB OFF ONTO THE BLANK BOX?

Sometimes things can "rub off" on us, too! Think about the music you listen to, the shows you watch and the games you play. Do you ever find yourself acting like those things?

Our minds absorb everything! And then our words and actions reflect the stuff we put into our minds! Write below about how imitating bad influences can affect your walk with Jesus.

Read <u>Philippians 4:8,</u> below and (circle) every word in all **CAPITAL** letters.

"And now, dear brothers and sisters, one final thing. Fix your thoughts on what is TRUE, and HONORABLE, and RIGHT, and PURE, and LOVELY, and ADMIRABLE. Think about things that are EXCELLENT and WORTHY OF PRAISE."

How many words did you circle?_____

WORLD CHANGER CHALLENGE:
Think about the things you watch, read, listen to, games you play, even the apps on your phone or tablet. Do they pass the **PHILIPPIANS 4:8 TEST?**

If you know that you are enjoying things that are not helping you follow Jesus and love Him with all your heart, gather those items together and ask your family to help you get rid of them, delete them, or donate them.

☑ TRUE
☑ HONORABLE
☑ RIGHT
☑ PURE
☑ LOVELY
☑ ADMIRABLE
☑ EXCELLENT
☑ WORTHY OF PRAISE

WELCOME TO DAY #5 OF CHANGING YOUR WORLD!!

You've come so far already! In the last four days we've learned about changing our **hearts**, **priorities**, **attitudes**, and **minds**.

Those four things are a big deal when it comes to changing your world because they are the foundation for everything else we will learn. Especially with today and tomorrow's topics.

Today we are focusing on our **WORDS**. Words can be helpful or hurtful. Make a list in the box below of some kind words.

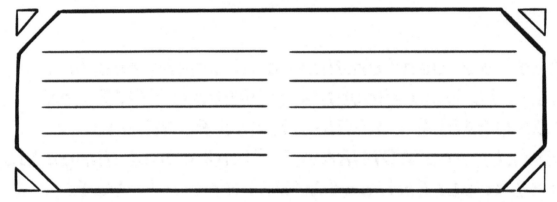

Let's be honest. Do you think about **EVERY** word you use **EVERY** day? Think about the words you've used lately, then fill in the scale and give your words a score.

WORDS MATTER!

The tongue can bring death or life...
Proverbs 18:21a

CAN YOU BELIEVE IT? Your words have power to build people up or tear them down! Your words can **CHANGE THE WORLD!** Take a look at these other verses and see what the Bible says about our words.

"Get rid of all bitterness, rage, anger, **HARSH WORDS**, and slander, as well as all types of evil behavior. Instead, be kind to each other, tenderhearted, forgiving one another, just as God through Christ has forgiven you." Ephesians 4:31-32

"So encourage each other and **BUILD EACH OTHER UP**, just as you are already doing." 1 Thessalonians 5:11

"**KIND WORDS ARE LIKE HONEY**-sweet to the soul and healthy for the body." Proverbs 16:24

"Don't use foul or abusive language. Let everything you say be good and helpful, so that **YOUR WORDS WILL BE AN ENCOURAGEMENT** to those who hear them." Ephesians 4:29

WORLD CHANGER CHALLENGE: Pick your favorite verse from the ones listed above and write it on a piece of paper and put it someplace you will see it AND read it **ALOUD** every day.

In the box below write the name of one person you are going to focus on encouraging and being kind to with your words.

TODAY IS AN AMAZING DAY! IT'S DAY #6

Hello World Changer! You are doing such a great job learning about God and becoming the **WORLD CHANGER** God has planned for you to be!

Today we are looking at our **ACTIONS!** Perhaps you've heard of the term, "behavior." Maybe you've even been told to behave yourself! Behavior is another word for our actions.

Our actions show a lot about what our **HEART** is like, where our **PRIORITIES** lie, our **ATTITUDE** and what we've allowed into our **MIND**! (Remember Days 1-4?) What's on the inside shows itself on the outside through our actions!

Have you ever had problems behaving? Maybe you have trouble sitting still, keeping your hands to yourself, or have even thrown a tantrum? It's possible you need to show **SELF-CONTROL!**

Let's do a little exercise. In the spaces below write your name using your left hand and then using your right hand.

LEFT HAND	RIGHT HAND
- - - - - - - - - -	- - - - - - - - - -

I bet one side looks a lot better than the other! Which hand was easier? _____ That hand is your *dominant* hand, which means that you have more control over it. Does that make your other hand useless? Not at all! But you do have less control over it in some areas, like writing.

In a way, that's how we are. With some things it's easier to have self-control. With others it's harder. For example, it may be easy for you to obey your parents, but hard using kind words.

The truth is it's impossible to be 100% perfect with our words or actions! Like we learned back in Day #1 we all miss the mark sometimes. **BUT DON'T GIVE UP!** When we struggle with our words or actions, Jesus is here to help us!

When we feel like we are about to lose self-control, and sin, that's called **TEMPTATION.** It's not a sin to be tempted. Jesus himself was tempted, but he never sinned, and he wants to help you when you're tempted, too. Check this out!

> God is faithful. He will not allow the temptation to be more than you can stand. When you are tempted, he will show you a way out so that you can endure.
> 1 Corinthians 10:13b

So, the next time you're tempted to sin, who should you go to for help?

WORLD CHANGER CHALLENGE: In your life you will be tempted to do, say, or think something you shouldn't. And you need help fighting those temptations. In the space below write a prayer asking Jesus to help you when you're tempted.

WELCOME TO DAY #7 WORLD CHANGER!

It is an amazing day! Right now, where you are, say this out loud...***"I AM A WORLD CHANGER!"*** You are created by God to do amazing things, right now! Isn't that amazing?

In the path to being a World Changer you will face challenges. Imagine the brave knights and soldiers you have read about in fairy tales. What did they have when they went off to fight in the battle? **ARMOR** and **WEAPONS.**

Guess what? Christians have armor and weapons too!

Read this verse from Ephesians 6:10-11

"A final word: Be strong in the Lord and in his mighty power. Put on all of God's armor so that you will be able to stand firm against all strategies of the devil."

So cool! God has armor just for Christians to wear! What is it? Grab your **BIBLE** and read Ephesians 6:13-17 to find out!

WOW!! WHAT DOES ALL THAT MEAN?

We have an enemy that does not want us to be **WORLD CHANGERS** and will try to discourage us. We receive our armor the moment we ask Jesus into our heart! But it's up to us to wear it! Can you imagine a soldier going out to battle without his armor and weapons? He wouldn't last long would he?

Check out the **SOLDIER** on the other page to see how your armor works!

- **BELT OF TRUTH-**We know God loves us and is for us!
- **BODY ARMOR OF GOD'S RIGHTEOUSNESS-**We know we are children of God!
- **SHOES OF PEACE-**We know Jesus and His salvation- That's Good News!
- **SHIELD OF FAITH-**We believe and trust God's Word!
- **HELMET OF SALVATION-** We know our sins have been forgiven!
- **SWORD OF THE SPIRIT-**We have God's Word, the Bible, to guide us & teach us!

So how do we put on our armor? Look at the first five in the list. All this armor comes from knowing who God is and what he's done for you. We can only be that close to God by having a friendship with Jesus and daily time in his presence. Now look at the sword. What is it? **YOUR BIBLE!** The more you read God's word the bigger of a threat you are to our enemy, the Devil, and the more you can change your world!

WORLD CHANGER CHALLENGE: God has given us weapons to use but it is our job to actually use them. With a parent's help and permission, get some cardboard or poster board and make a sword and shield. You can use aluminum foil to decorate them. Use a marker and write **I AM A WORLD CHANGER** on them to remind yourself of who you are!

Make sure you put them in a place you can see them every day!
YOU ARE A WORLD CHANGER!

WORLD CHANGER WRAP-UP WEEK #1

All this week you have been working really hard on becoming an amazing World Changer! You've learned how to change your heart, priorities, attitude, mind, words, and actions. Yesterday you learned about the armor and weapons God has given you to help you change your world!

What has this week taught you about yourself?

What area was the **HARDEST** for you?

HEART		PRIORITIES
ATTITUDE	MIND	WORDS
ACTIONS		ARMOR OF GOD

Why do you think it was so hard?

HOW DO YOU FEEL WHEN YOU THINK OF YOURSELF AS A WORLD CHANGER?

God has special plans and jobs that only you can do.
- If you are quiet & shy...**YOU ARE A WORLD CHANGER!**
- If you are loud & outgoing...**YOU ARE A WORLD CHANGER!**
- If you love animals...**YOU ARE A WORLD CHANGER!**
- If you love sports, ice cream, reading, video games, movies, music, all the above or none of the above...**GUESS WHAT!**

YOU ARE A WORLD CHANGER!

In the space below, in your own words, thank God for choosing you to be a World Changer, and ask God to help you do all that he has planned for you to do and then thank Him for helping you finish the first week so strong.

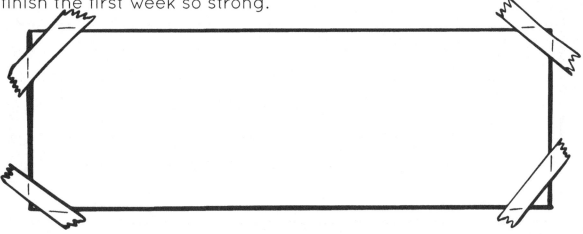

WRITE ABOUT WEEK 1 HERE

WEEK 1 DOODLE PAGE!

NO. 2

THINGS I'M PRAYING ABOUT THIS WEEK...

NO. 2

WEEK 2
CHANGE YOUR ATMOSPHERE

This week you will continue changing the world by...

- [ ] Changing your **HOME**
- [ ] Changing your **SIBLINGS**
- [ ] Changing your **FRIENDS**
- [ ] Changing your **RELATIONSHIPS**
- [ ] Changing your **ENEMIES**
- [ ] Changing your **SCHOOL**
- [ ] Changing your **CHURCH**

WELCOME TO DAY #8 WORLD CHANGER!!

Today is a wonderful day and you are going to do awesome things! **YOU ARE A WORLD CHANGER!!**

Ready for today's focus? Today is about changing your **HOME.** That doesn't mean you are packing up and moving to a different place, but it means changing the **ATMOSPHERE** of your home.

What does that even mean? Here is some help. Every day we are in different atmospheres or places that feel different, like happy or grumpy, calm or chaotic.

Imagine shopping with your family. Would you enjoy a store that is crowded, dirty, with hard to find items, and full of angry people? Most likely not. Would you enjoy a store that is clean, calm, with easy to find items, and with friendly people to help you? Absolutely! The stores could sell the same things but it is the atmosphere that makes the difference.

WHAT IS THE ATMOSPHERE IN YOUR HOME? Circle the words that describe it best.

FRIENDLY   KIND   ANGRY   CALM

LOUD   BUSY   HELPFUL   LOVING   MESSY

CLEAN   HAPPY   PEACEFUL   SAD

NOISY   QUIET

Do you know that ***YOU*** can help with the atmosphere of your home? You can and it is pretty easy! Want to learn the trick?

HONORING YOUR MOTHER AND FATHER.

Check out this verse from God's Word.

> "Honor your father and mother," This is the first commandment with a promise. If you honor your father and mother, "things will go well with you, and you will have a long life on the earth."
> Ephesians 6:2-3

Did you hear that? If you honor (obey, listen to, respect) your parents you will have a great and long life!

WORLD CHANGER CHALLENGE: Think about how you talk to your parents. What kind of words do you use? Do you argue back or do you listen and obey? Check the following areas and use a **+** if you do it well or a **-** if you need improvement in that area. Be honest!!!

You do chores without arguing or delay.	
You do things without being told (getting dressed, brushing your teeth, cleaning your room, etc.)	
You see a need and help meet a need that your family has.	
You don't fuss or whine if you don't get your way.	
You accept decisions your family makes without arguing, even if you don't like it.	

Pray about the areas that you gave yourself a **-** and ask God to help you honor your parents every day.

IT'S DAY #9-HELLO WORLD CHANGER!

You are doing a great job learning to be a World Changer! You are amazing!

Today is going to be so much fun! The focus is all about changing our **SIBLINGS** (also known as your brothers and sisters)!

YOU PROBABLY HAVE A FEW QUESTIONS...

 Can I can physically change my siblings into something else, like a cute puppy?

I don't have siblings, what do I do?

 You haven't met my siblings, they are crazy. How am I going to change them?

EXCELLENT QUESTIONS!

 No, you cannot change your siblings into something or someone else, make them disappear or turn them into a pet.

If you don't have any siblings then imagine that this lesson applies to people really close to you. It could be your parents again, friends, classmates, other family members... anyone.

IF YOU DO HAVE SIBLINGS, TAKE A DEEP BREATH, YOU CAN DO IT! YOU ARE A WORLD CHANGER AFTER ALL!

> "Love is patient and kind. Love is not jealous or boastful or proud or rude. It does not demand its own way. It is not irritable, and it keeps no record of being wronged. It does not rejoice about injustice but rejoices whenever truth wins out. Love never gives up, never loses faith, is always hopeful, and endures through every circumstance."
> 1 Corinthians 13: 4-7

What word did you notice written over and over again?

L♡VE

WORLD CHANGER CHALLENGE: This verse shows us a lot of things that love is and some things it isn't. Read the verse again and fill in the chart below with things that love is or does and isn't or doesn't do.

LOVE IS/DOES...	LOVE ISN'T/DOESN'T...

Spend time praying and asking God to help you love your siblings, or others in your family, more, then look for ways to show them love. **YOU CAN DO THIS!**

IT'S A WONDERFUL DAY- WELCOME TO DAY #10

You are a World Changer, created by God to do amazing things- today! At the age you are now! Isn't that exciting? You are doing an amazing job!

Today our focus is on changing our **FRIENDS.** This one may be challenging but you will be great!

Friends are so important! They are lots of fun, they can help us when we face problems, laugh at our jokes, and care for us. Some friendships are helpful, but some friendships are hurtful.

We want to choose friends that will **ENCOURAGE** us to be World Changers and to love God with all our hearts.

Make a list of what you think makes someone a **GOOD FRIEND.**

Check out what God's Word says about friends.

Proverbs 26:18-19 "Just as damaging as a **MADMAN** shooting a deadly weapon is someone who lies to a friend and then says, **"I WAS ONLY JOKING."**

THAT DOES NOT SOUND LIKE A GOOD FRIEND AT ALL!

<u>Proverbs 18:24</u> "There are "friends" who destroy each other, but a **REAL FRIEND** sticks closer than a brother."

Just like a family member, a real friend will be with you no matter what.

Good friends are such a blessing!

WORLD CHANGER CHALLENGE: Guess what? God has put you in your world for a reason, to share Jesus with people around you. Being a World Changer also means being a great friend, loving people all around you, like you learned on Day #9.

To change the world you need to be out in the world. Nothing gets changed if you are hiding under your bed, right?

Think about the friends you have and think about these questions.

Do any of them already **LOVE JESUS?** They should be your closest or best friends.

Do any of them **NEED** to hear about Jesus? Think about how you can tell them how much Jesus loves them, or how you can invite them to church.

Do any of them need **HELP** or **ENCOURAGEMENT?** Think of what you can do to help.

Do any of them need God's help? Think of ways you can **PRAY** for them.

Use the next few pages to help you make your list.

FRIENDS WHO LOVE JESUS:

FRIENDS WHO NEED TO KNOW ABOUT JESUS:

FRIENDS WHO NEED ENCOURAGEMENT OR HELP:

FRIENDS I CAN PRAY FOR:

WELCOME TO DAY #11 WORLD CHANGER!

Today is a great day! God created you on purpose and with a purpose! You are a World Changer! Isn't that exciting? You are doing an amazing job!

Today our focus is on changing our **RELATIONSHIPS.** But what relationships and with whom? Great question! The focus today is on all the people you see often but maybe aren't your friends. There is a fancy word for those people, they are called **ACQUAINTANCES.** Think of people like your bus driver, your teachers, your neighbors, or anyone else you see often and maybe even know their name, but you wouldn't say they are your friends. Use the space below and make a list of people you know that might fit in this category.

Great job on your list! Now you may be wondering, how can I change those relationships? Let's check out God's Word for the answer.

"Since God chose you to be the holy people he loves, you must clothe yourselves with tenderhearted mercy, kindness, humility, gentleness, and patience. Make allowance for each other's faults, and forgive anyone who offends you...Above all, clothe yourself with love, which binds us all together in perfect harmony."
Colossians 3:12-14

Make a list of the attributes from this verse that are important to show to others. Hint, there are **EIGHT** of them!

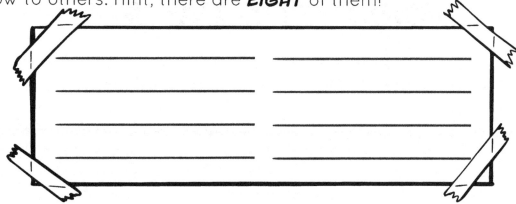

Because you love Jesus with all of your heart, that love should be seen in how you treat people. Those you love and those you don't know well. In fact, even people you don't like at all!

Being a **WORLD CHANGER** means looking and sounding different than other people, showing forgiveness, patience, and love.

WORLD CHANGER CHALLENGE:

Look at the list of people that you wrote of people that would be **ACQUAINTANCES**. Think about how you can encourage them or show kindness to them in some way. Maybe writing a thank you note or giving a small treat to show appreciation. Get a blank piece of paper and draw a heart like this one here. You can decorate the page with the attributes that you listed from today's verse. Color in a piece of heart for each act of kindness that you do for someone. How quickly can you fill the heart up?

YOU ARE CHANGING THE WORLD—IT'S DAY #12!

How does it feel being a World Changer? What things have you noticed changing in your world? Take a moment and write about that below.

Today we are focusing on changing our **ENEMIES.** An enemy can be anyone you don't like or who you know doesn't like you. On Day #6 we talked about self-control. While you can't control how someone feels about you, but **YOU CAN CONTROL** your response to them and how you treat them.

Let's see what God's Word says about enemies.

Luke 6:27-28 (This is Jesus talking) "But to you who are willing to listen, I say, **LOVE YOUR ENEMIES!** Do good to those who hate you. Bless those who curse you. Pray for those who hurt you."

Jesus goes on to say in Luke 6:31 "Do to others as you would like them to do to you."

THAT'S AMAZING! Jesus wants us to love the people who don't like us, show kindness to them and pray for them. That could be a really **BIG JOB.**

GRAB YOUR BIBLE AND READ LUKE 10:30-37.

Of all the people in the story, which person showed kindness to the hurt man? Circle the correct answer!

ROBBERS   **PRIEST**   **TEMPLE ASSISTANT**   **SAMARITAN**

What is amazing in this story is that the Samaritan knew that the Jewish man didn't like him and considered him an **ENEMY.**

Did that stop him from showing love and kindness? _____

WORLD CHANGER CHALLENGE: You are a World Changer and that is pretty SUPER! In fact, this challenge is a SUPER CHALLENGE. In the space below draw your own **SUPER WORLD CHANGER LOGO.** On the lines provided, write down the name of anyone you may consider an enemy, and ways you can pray for them and then commit to praying for them every day.

HELLO WORLD CHANGER!
IT'S DAY #13

You are doing amazing! All week you have been focusing on changing the world around you and we continue today with changing your **SCHOOL!** Maybe you have a big school with lots of kids in your class or you are home-schooled all by yourself... guess what? **YOU CAN STILL CHANGE YOUR SCHOOL!**

Every school has the same things in common, there are teachers and people who help you learn. The job of a teacher is **HUGE!** Teachers help us learn new things and make us smarter people. Imagine what it is like being *your* teacher with *your* class. Use the scale below to grade how easy or hard that job would be.

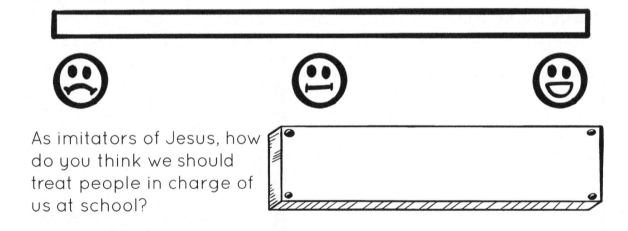

As imitators of Jesus, how do you think we should treat people in charge of us at school?

CHECK OUR WHAT GOD'S WORD SAY ABOUT IT.

"Everyone must submit to governing authorities. For all authority comes from God, and those in positions of authority have been placed there by God."
Romans 13:1

Does this mean you need to obey your teacher? **YES!**
What about obeying the principal? **YES AGAIN!**
The lunch lady? The teacher with recess duty? The librarian?
YES TO ALL THOSE!

God has placed you at your school, with your teacher and school leaders for a reason: so you can **SHINE YOUR LIGHT** and show God's love and kindness in that place. It is a job only **YOU** can do!

LET'S LOOK AT ONE MORE VERSE.

> "So encourage each other and build each other up." - 1 Thessalonians 5:11

God's Word is telling us to obey those in charge of us and encourage and build them up.

•	How can you change your school?
•	What if your teacher is having a hard day?
•	What if you don't like an assignment?
•	What if you don't want to follow instructions?
•	What if the teacher needs some help?
•	**ANSWER: OBEY AND BE AN ENCOURAGER!**

WORLD CHANGER CHALLENGE: Write a thank you note to your teacher or teachers at school. Thank them for all they do for you and for the school and let them know you are praying for them. Then commit to praying for your school everyday. Pray for your class, for the teachers and for all the people who lead your school. Making BIG decisions is a hard job and they need lots of wisdom.

YOU ARE CHANGING THE WORLD! WELCOME TO DAY #14

Hello World Changer! God is using you in a HUGE WAY to change the world around you. You are showing God's love and kindness and it is making a **HUGE DIFFERENCE!**

Today we are focusing on changing our **CHURCH!** Hopefully you have a church that you love and attend. If you don't go to church, talk to your family and ask them about attending a local church this week.

God loves his people, and the place where his people gather together is called the church. It's God's House!

How can we change our church? Let's see what God's Word says.

Psalm 69:9 "Passion for your house has consumed me."

Here is how this verse breaks down. **PASSION** is a word that shows strong feelings. **HOUSE** is referring to the Church, not just the building, but also the **PEOPLE** who gather to worship and learn about God.

So in this verse we see that we should have strong feelings and love for God's House. How do we do that?

We can do that by...

 Serving and helping at our church.

 Praying for our church and our pastors.

 Inviting people to our church to hear more about God's love for them.

God's House is full of God's people and God **LOVES** his people.

WORLD CHANGER CHALLENGE: Write some things below that you love about your church.

I LOVE MY CHURCH BECAUSE...

MY FAVORITE PART OF GOING TO CHURCH IS...

I WANT TO PRAY EVERY DAY FOR MY PASTORS. THEIR NAMES ARE ...

I CAN DO THIS TO HELP OUT AT MY CHURCH ...

I CAN INVITE THIS FRIEND TO CHURCH WITH ME ...

WORLD CHANGER WRAP-UP WEEK #2

All this week you have been working really hard on becoming an amazing World Changer! You've learned how to change your home, siblings, friends, relationships, enemies, school, and church!

What has this week taught you about yourself?

What area was the **HARDEST** for you?

HOME	SIBLINGS

FRIENDS	RELATIONSHIPS	ENEMIES

SCHOOL	CHURCH

Why do you think it was so hard?

HOW DO YOU FEEL WHEN YOU THINK OF YOURSELF AS A WORLD CHANGER?

God has special plans and jobs that only you can do.
- If you are quiet & shy...**YOU ARE A WORLD CHANGER!**
- If you are loud & outgoing...**YOU ARE A WORLD CHANGER!**
- If you love animals...**YOU ARE A WORLD CHANGER!**
- If you love sports, ice cream, reading, video games, movies, music, all the above or none of the above...**GUESS WHAT!**

YOU ARE A WORLD CHANGER!

In the space below, in your own words, thank God for choosing you to be a World Changer, and ask God to help you do all that he has planned for you to do and then thank Him for helping you finish the second week so strong.

WRITE ABOUT WEEK 2 HERE

WEEK 2 DOODLE PAGE!

NO. 2

WEEK 3
CHANGE YOUR WORLD

This week you will finish changing the world by...

- [ ] Changing your **NEIGHBORHOOD**
- [ ] Changing your **COMMUNITY**
- [ ] Changing your **STATE**
- [ ] Changing your **COUNTRY**
- [ ] Changing your **WORLD**
- [ ] Reading **GOD'S WORD**
- [ ] **PRAYER**

IT'S DAY #15 OF CHANGING THE WORLD

Hello awesome World Changer! God is using you in **HUGE** ways to change the world around you. It might not feel like much, but it is making a difference. Your actions and kindness is showing others God's love and encouraging them to become **WORLD CHANGERS** too!

Today we are going to learn how you can change your **NEIGHBORHOOD.** Do you live in a place with lots of people around you, like an apartment or a neighborhood, or do you have less people that live close to you? **WHO ARE YOUR NEIGHBORS?** Write the names of your neighbors. If you don't know your neighbors' names you can ask your parents, or use descriptive names like "The nice people with the fluffy dog," or "That lady with all those cats!" Write as many as you can remember.

MY NEIGHBORS

God knows where you live and who lives in the homes around you. God sees all people and He knows if they are happy or sad, having a good day or a terrible day. **GOD LOVES PEOPLE SO MUCH,** even the ones who don't love Him back yet. God wants to reach the lost, people who don't know about Jesus. He could send an army of angels, or talk to them with a voice from the heavens but God doesn't do that. **GOD USES PEOPLE** who love him, like you do, to tell others about Jesus.

HOW CAN GOD USE YOU TO SHARE JESUS WITH YOUR NEIGHBORS?

> "You must love the Lord your God with all your heart, all your soul, all your strength, and all your mind." And, "Love your neighbor as yourself."
> Luke 10:27

God's Word tells us to love our **NEIGHBOR** just like we love ourselves. What are some ways that you love and care for yourself? (Think of how you take care of yourself.)

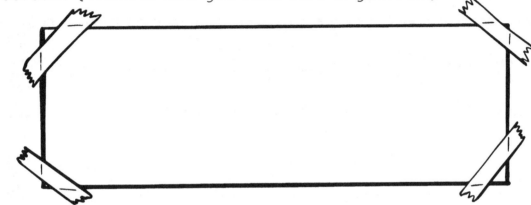

Does this mean we have to go to each house around us and make sure people are getting dressed and brushing their teeth? No, that's silly. It's a simple as **TREATING OTHERS THE SAME WAY YOU WANT TO BE TREATED,** praying for their needs, and telling them about how Jesus has changed your life!

WORLD CHANGER CHALLENGE:
Look at your list of neighbors. It could seem like a LOT of work to love and care for each of them all at once. But changing your neighborhood happens one person at a time. Talk with your parents and pray about how you can show ONE neighbor the love of Jesus. It could be as simple as having a conversation with someone, or delivering cookies, an invitation to church, or doing a chore for an elderly or disabled neighbor.
YOU CAN CHANGE YOUR NEIGHBORHOOD!

HELLO WORLD CHANGER!
IT'S DAY #16

The world around you is becoming more awesome because you are **CHANGING YOUR WORLD!**

Today the focus is on changing your **COMMUNITY,** the town or city where you live. Take some time right now to write about your community; its name, and places you love to go, play, eat and have fun.

MY COMMUNITY'S NAME: _____

PLACES IN MY COMMUNITY I LIKE TO VISIT:

Today we are looking at ways to **SHARE JESUS** with the community around you. When you love Jesus with all your heart, you have His love in you and you are like a light shining in a dark room.

What happens when you go into a dark room? Do you just walk around in darkness? No, you turn on a light. The Bible refers to people who don't know Jesus as people walking in darkness. They need to see the light of Jesus. But how can they see the light? Hint: **YOU CAN HELP SHINE A LIGHT!**

"You are the light of the world—like a city on a hilltop that cannot be hidden. No one lights a lamp and then puts it under a basket. Instead, a lamp is placed on a stand, where it gives light to everyone in the house. In the same way, let your good deeds shine out for all to see, so that everyone will praise your heavenly Father.
Matthew 5:14-16

How can our community see the light of Jesus? When we **LOVE GOD AND LOVE OTHERS** with our words and actions, we shine the light of Jesus brighter than a big city at night!

WORLD CHANGER CHALLENGE: Talk to your family about ways you can get involved and help your community. Pray together about what you can do to change your community. Here are some ideas to help you.

 Does your community have a **food pantry** that feeds people? Collect food to donate to the pantry.

 Spend an afternoon **cleaning up trash** in a local park.

 Does your community have an **animal shelter**? Donate pet food or time to help the shelter.

 Take a walk and spend time **praying** for your community.

WHEN YOU LET YOUR LIGHT SHINE IN YOUR COMMUNITY YOU ARE A WORLD CHANGER!

WELCOME TO DAY #17 WORLD CHANGER!

Today is a great day! God created you on purpose and with a purpose! You are a World Changer! At the age you are now! Isn't that exciting? **YOU ARE DOING AN AMAZING JOB!**

You have been working so hard at changing the world around you. Don't give up! Keep up the great work. You are making a **HUGE** difference!

Today the focus is on your **STATE, PROVINCE, REGION, DISTRICT, OR TERRITORY.** That sounds like a lot of places, but depending on the country you live in, it may be called something different. For example, the United States has states, and Canada has provinces. If you don't know what you have you can ask your parents for help. Write your state (or province, etc) below.

I LIVE IN THE _____ OF _____

Guess what? Your state is awesome! God has placed lots of men and women in special jobs to help make your state a better place? There are people that are in charge of keeping the roads you drive on safe and in good condition. There are people that help make the laws. There are people that help keep the parks clean and care for the animals. There are even people whose job it is to represent your state in your country's government.

Running a state is a **HUGE JOB** and as Christians one of the most important things we can do is to **PRAY** for the people who help are responsible for our state!

> "I urge you, first of all, to pray for all people. Ask God to help them; intercede on their behalf, and give thanks for them. Pray this way for kings and all who are in authority..."
> 1 Timothy 2:1-2a

When we pray for our state leaders we are asking God to help them make important decisions and laws, and asking God to give them wisdom to make the right choices. When we actively pray for the leaders of our state, we are **CHANGING THE WORLD** we live in.

WORLD CHANGER CHALLENGE: Ask your family to help you look up and fill in the answers below.

MY STATE'S LEADERS ARE... (this could include your governor, representatives, senators, or other government leaders.)

_____   _____

_____   _____

_____   _____

Now follow the 1 Timothy 2 model.

PRAY-Commit to praying for these leaders by name and asking God to help them make good decisions as they lead. Pray that they have a relationship with Jesus and will love God with all their hearts.

GIVE THANKS-Write a thank you note to one of the people above and thank them for all they are doing to make your state so awesome. Tell them you are praying for them. Don't forget to mail it!

YOU ARE A WORLD CHANGER! IT'S DAY #18

You are doing amazing! All week you have been focusing on changing your neighborhood, community, and state. Can you guess what we are changing today? You guessed it! We continue today with changing our **COUNTRY!**

Just like your state, your country has people that are in charge of different areas to make it a great place to live. It is a **REALLY BIG JOB** to run a country.

Imagine if you were in charge of the country for a day. What laws would you want to make or change? Make your list below.

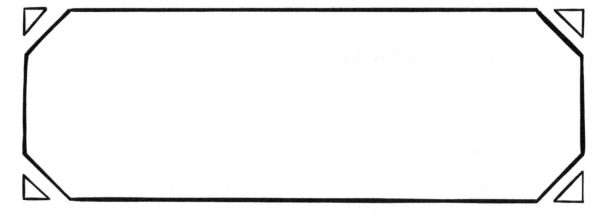

The people who work in the government have lots of **RESPONSIBILITIES.** They think about keeping people safe and healthy. They think about the best way to spend money. They think about the best laws to make to help people. It is a lot of work and can be really hard because they have to think about so many people. They need lots and lots of wisdom!!

GOD HAS AN AMAZING PLAN FOR THE LIVES OF YOUR GOVERNMENT LEADERS! He placed them in their position, and they need your support and prayers to do their job.

> "Everyone must submit to governing authorities. For all authority comes from God, and those in positions of authority have been placed there by God."
> Romans 13:1

Throughout your life you will have government leaders that you will like and others you won't. But your job as a Christian is always to **HONOR**, **OBEY**, and **PRAY FOR THEM**.

WHEN YOU DO THIS, GUESS WHAT...YOU ARE CHANGING THE WORLD!

WORLD CHANGER CHALLENGE: Today we are going to repeat yesterday's challenge, this time for your country, so you may need to ask your family to help you fill in the answers below.

MY COUNTRY'S LEADERS ARE... (this could include your president, vice-president, prime minister, king, or queen)

PRAY-Commit to praying for these leaders by name and asking God to help them make good decisions as they lead. Pray that they have a relationship with Jesus and will love God with all their hearts.

GIVE THANKS-Write a thank you note to one of the people above and thank them for all they are doing to make your state so awesome. Tell them you are praying for them. Don't forget to mail it!

HEY THERE, WORLD CHANGER! IT'S DAY #19

What an amazing week! Your prayers for your world are making a huge difference. Check out this verse from God's Word.

> "The earnest prayer of a righteous person has great power and produces wonderful results."
> James 5:16b

When we ask God into our hearts we become a righteous person. This verse says that when we pray, our prayers have great power and produce results! Your prayers for your world are making a difference! Don't stop praying for those leaders!

Today we are expanding our focus even further, can you guess what's next? That's right...**THE ENTIRE WORLD!**

Make a list of some other countries you have heard about or even visited before.

God created the world and everything in it, all the plants, animals, and people. He loves the world and all the people of the world. He made each person, with different looks and skin colors, with different talents and skills, and **EACH PERSON IS SPECIAL.**

God loves all people and wants them to all have their sins forgiven too. Take a look at this verse.

> "And then he [Jesus] told them, "Go into all the world and preach the Good News to everyone." - Mark 16:15

Just like you can tell people in your family, school, neighborhood, and community about Jesus, there are people who go into different countries all over the world to tell people about Jesus. Those people are called **MISSIONARIES.**

A missionary does exactly what Mark 16:15 says, they preach Jesus, and what he did on the Cross, to people all over the world. It is a great job but can also be really hard. They have to learn a new language, new customs or ways people live, they learn to eat strange foods and live in different homes. They also may have to live away from their friends and families. They give up a lot to do what God has called them to do.

Do you think missionaries need our prayers? **ABSOLUTELY!**

Do you think they need our help? **YOU BET!**

BUT HOW CAN YOU HELP?

Flip the page to our **SUPER WORLD CHANGER CHALLENGE** to see how you can help missionaries and be a HUGE part of **CHANGING THE WORLD!**

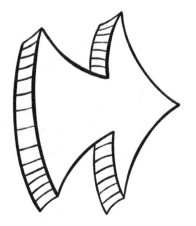

SUPER WORLD CHANGER CHALLENGE:

Talk to your pastor at church about **MISSIONARIES** your church helps and learn more about them. Find out their names and what country they are missionaries to. Consider doing one of the following to help **SUPPORT** your missionaries.

POST CARD

2¢
U.S. Pos

COMMIT TO PRAYING FOR YOUR CHURCH'S MISSIONARIES AND THE PEOPLE OF THAT COUNTRY. ASK GOD TO GIVE THEM FAVOR, PROVIDE FOR THEIR NEEDS, AND TO HELP THEM SHARE JESUS WITH THE PEOPLE. ALSO, ASK GOD TO PROTECT THEM AND KEEP THEM IN GREAT HEALTH.

TO: _____

_____

_____

_____

POST CARD

RAISE MONEY FOR MISSIONARIES. Ask your family if you can do extra jobs or chores to help raise money to send to help missionaries. You can also make cookies or crafts to sell and raise money. Give that money to the church to help the missionaries they support.

_____

_____

_____

_____

POST CARD

<u>HOST A MISSIONARY DINNER.</u>
Make food from the country that your missionary is in and invite your friends and family. You can teach them about the country during the dinner. You can even play games that kids play in that country. Close your dinner by praying for the missionaries and for the people in that country.

TO: _____

_____

_____

_____

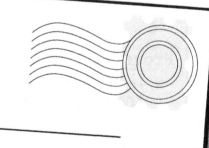

<u>FIND OUT ABOUT MISSION TRIPS</u>
<u>YOUR CHURCH MAY BE DOING</u> AND PRAY ABOUT BEING A PART OF THE TRIP WITH YOUR FAMILY. MISSION TRIPS ALLOW YOU TO GO TO A MISSION FIELD, AND HELP THE MISSIONARIES WITH PROJECTS THEY ARE WORKING ON. SOMETIMES KIDS CAN GO ON TRIPS WITH THEIR FAMILIES, BUT IF NOT YOU MAY BE ABLE TO HELP SPONSOR A FRIEND OR CHURCH MEMBER WHO HAS SIGNED UP FOR A MISSION TRIP.

_____

_____

_____

_____

WOW, WORLD CHANGER! IT'S DAY #20

You are 100% a **WORLD CHANGER!** You have walked through so many places in your world and looked at ways to make them a better place. You have done an amazing job, but you aren't done yet.

The world still needs you. The world needs you to love God with all your heart. So today's focus is all about **GOD'S WORD, THE BIBLE.**

TAKE A MOMENT TO READ THESE VERSES ABOUT GOD'S WORD <u>OUT LOUD!</u>

Deuteronomy 8:3b-People do not live by bread alone; rather, we live by every word that comes from the mouth of the Lord.

Proverbs 30:5-Every word of God proves true. He is a shield to all who come to him for protection.

2 Timothy 3:16-All Scripture is inspired by God and is useful to teach us what is true and to make us realize what is wrong in our lives. It corrects us when we are wrong and teaches us to do what is right.

Psalm 119:105-Your word is a lamp to guide my feet and a light for my path.

The Bible shows us who God is, what God is like, and how very much God loves and cares for us. To be followers of Jesus we need to know about God and what His Word says.

Just like we learned on Day #7 our Bibles are also known as the **SWORD OF THE SPIRIT.** Can you imagine a soldier going out to battle without taking his sword? He wouldn't last very long. Our Bible is like a sword that helps us when we are tempted, sad, worried or uncertain.

Grab your Bible and read the story in **MATTHEW 4:1-11**, to see how Jesus used God's Word like a sword!

Jesus was able to fight temptation and the enemy's attack because He knew God's Word so well. We can follow that same example and know God's Word too, so we can fight the enemy like Jesus did!

WORLD CHANGER CHALLENGE: Grab your Bible and get familiar with the Table of Contents. Reading the Bible is not like reading any other book, you don't have to start on Page 1 and read to the end.

The Bible is divided into two sections, the **OLD TESTAMENT** and the **NEW TESTAMENT.** The Old Testament starts with Creation and is the story of God's People before the birth of Jesus. The New Testament begins with the birth of **JESUS,** his life, death, and resurrection, as well as the first **CHURCH,** and several books written by Jesus' disciples about how to best follow Jesus.

Find a Bible **READING PLAN** that works for you and spend time reading through God's Word. Read with a notebook, a pen, and a highlighter so you can write about and mark verses that stand out to you. Ask your parents or kids' pastor for help with this and keep your plan simple so you can accomplish your goal.

YOU ARE A WORLD CHANGER—IT'S DAY #21!!!

IT'S DAY #21...THE LAST DAY! You have done an amazing job becoming a World Changer! Give yourself a round of applause right now! God is using you to change the world around you and will continue to use you in huge ways! There is one final thing that is a huge part of being a World Changer. **ARE YOU READY?**

Today the focus is on **PRAYER, TALKING TO GOD.**

God loves to talk to his people and loves it when his people talk to him. Think about your best friend. Do you talk to that person very much? Of course you do! When someone is important to you, you want to spend time talking to them.

God is not only our Heavenly Father, but is also our closest friend. So how can our friendship with God grow? By talking to Him!

AND GOD ABSOLUTELY LOVES HEARING FROM US!

> Because he [God] bends down to listen, I will pray as long as I have breath!
> Psalm 116:2

This verse tells us that God bends down, he gets close to us, every time we pray. Just like a grown-up bends down to hear a child speak, God gives us his full attention when we pray.

Grab your Bible and read **MATTHEW 6:9-13** to learn how Jesus taught his disciples to pray.

That might seem confusing but what Jesus gave us was a prayer model. We don't have to pray those exact words but rather follow the model using your own words.

WHAT JESUS SAID	WHAT IT MEANS
Our Father in heaven, may your name be kept holy.	Tell God you love him so much and spend some time praising and thanking him.
May your Kingdom come soon. May your will be done on earth, as it is in heaven.	Tell God you want His best for your life and ask that things happen in your life the way God wants them to.
Give us today the food we need.	Tell God what you need and that you trust him to meet your needs. Thank him for helping you.
And forgive us our sins, as we have forgiven those who sin against us.	Ask God to forgive you of your sins and help you to forgive others.
And don't let us yield to temptation.	Ask God to help keep you from sinning. Ask for special help in areas you're tempted the most.
But rescue us from the evil one.	Ask God to protect you and your family wherever you go.

God answers every prayer but it may not always look like we want. God knows us best and knows what we need better than we do, so we can always trust Him.

WORLD CHANGER CHALLENGE: Get a piece of poster board and some sticky notes. Divide the poster board into two columns, one titled **PRAYER NEEDS** and the other titled **PRAISE REPORTS.** Use the sticky notes to write down any prayer requests or the names of people you are praying for, then put them in the PRAYER NEEDS column. When God answers your prayer, move the sticky note to the PRAISE REPORT column!

WORLD CHANGER WRAP-UP
WEEK #3

All this week you have been working really hard on becoming an amazing World Changer! You've learned how to change your neighborhood, community, state, country, and the world! You also learned how God's Word and Prayer can help you be a World Changer!

What has this week taught you about yourself?

What area was the **HARDEST** for you?

NEIGHBORHOOD   COMMUNITY

STATE   COUNTRY   WORLD

GOD'S WORD   PRAYER

Why do you think it was so hard?

HOW DO YOU FEEL WHEN YOU THINK OF YOURSELF AS A WORLD CHANGER?

God has special plans and jobs that only you can do.

- If you are quiet & shy...**YOU ARE A WORLD CHANGER!**
- If you are loud & outgoing...**YOU ARE A WORLD CHANGER!**
- If you love animals...**YOU ARE A WORLD CHANGER!**
- If you love sports, ice cream, reading, video games, movies, music, all the above or none of the above...**GUESS WHAT!**

YOU ARE A WORLD CHANGER!

In the space below, in your own words, thank God for choosing you to be a World Changer, and ask God to help you do all that he has planned for you to do and then thank Him for helping you finish the third week so strong.

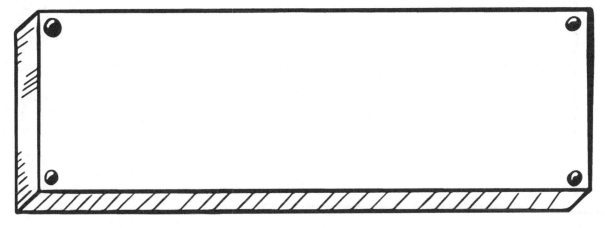

WRITE ABOUT WEEK 3 HERE

WEEK 3 DOODLE PAGE!

NO. 2

CONGRATULATIONS!
YOU ARE A WORLD CHANGER!

You have completed your **21-DAY WORLD CHANGER DEVOTIONAL,** but your journey has just begun! God has big plans for you and it's so exciting to think about what God has in store for your life, as you continue to change **YOURSELF,** your **ATMOSPHERE,** and even the **WORLD!**

This devotional has helped get you started on your World Changer journey, and it can continue to help you.

Every once in awhile pick this devotional up and read through it again. See how far God has taken you on your journey and make new notes to share how God is now using you to change your world!

REMEMBER:
You are God's Masterpiece!
God created you on purpose with a purpose!
God has big plans for your life!
You are a World Changer!

MANY BLESSINGS!

Made in the USA
Monee, IL
05 March 2020